EMPOWERED
WOMAN

The

WHAT PEOPLE ARE SAYING ABOUT *THE EMPOWERED WOMAN*

In *The Empowered Woman*, Marta Spirk does an amazing job of walking you through the steps to be comfortable in your own shoes at a level you never would've imagined possible. The seal of approval you will bestow on yourself after reading this book is nothing short of a blessing.

— CHRISTINA NICHOLSON, TV Host and Host of the *Become a Media Maven Podcast*

The Empowered Woman is the definition of taking a chance on yourself, going all-in, and moving from a place of faith instead of moving from a place of fear. It's inspiring to read about Marta's journey from being unsure of what gifts she'd contribute to the world to showing up as a powerhouse for herself, her family, and her audience.

— LISA SIMONE RICHARDS, PR and Visibility Strategist at LisaSimoneRichards.com

The Empowered Woman is a truly special book. Marta Spirk's courage is evident by her willingness to share both the ups and the downs of her personal journey, which has allowed her to become the empowered woman she has become. Marta is inviting you to follow the path she discovered to embrace the empowered woman you are. Trust her and she won't let you down. I also recommend this book to any man who wants to support the women he cares about.

— GARY BARNES, International Speaker, Serial Entrepreneur, and Traction Business Coach at GaryBarnesInternational.com

While reading *The Empowered Woman*, I felt like I was sitting with a dear friend who was baring her soul in a way that only friends can. But more than that, she was also sharing her vision and stepping more into *herself*, page after page. She is a lighthouse, and I know she is also lighting the way for women everywhere going through the dark season of unfulfilled purpose, showing them that they do have a bigger calling and with that calling, the ability to step into their power as women and entrepreneurs. I know I did!

— REBECA LIMA, Business Coach and Strategist at RebecaLima.Coach

Business success starts with knowing who we are. The fact that *The Empowered Woman* starts with a self-assessment tool, the Enneagram, sets the reader up for an empowering journey toward understanding their strengths and finding opportunities for growth. Marta helps you reflect on whether you are building a business that is aligned with who you are so you can ditch the masks and show up as *yourself*. The Empowered Woman Path puts us in the driver seat of our life!

— DAWN PENSACK, EFT Practitioner, Founder/CEO, Dawn Pensack Coaching

I was impressed when I read *The Empowered Woman* by Marta Spirk. As a journalist and working mom, this book moved me with its practical and personal insights about the desire to be perfect in today's society. Marta is a powerful example for female entrepreneurs and joyfully shows other women how to live their dreams and achieve success without fear. I recommend adding this book to your collection because it is filled with empowering stories that will inspire you.

— NATALIE TYSDAL, Host of *The Natalie Tysdal Podcast*, TV Anchor, Mom

If you put your 100% into something, you will get the most authentic and meaningful lessons from it. And in *The Empowered Woman*, Marta shows exactly that. When reading this book, you will navigate through the deepest lessons that Marta has learned throughout her journey, and your experience will surely be transformational and amazing!

— CAROLINA MELO, PhD in Business Economics, MPA in Development Practice

An inspiring, touching, unique life story that culminates with Marta becoming a guide who empowers women to find their real place in the world after overcoming difficulties and turning them into success.

— GLORIA DELBIM, English Language and Literature MA, Speaker, Translator

The Empowered Woman Path that Marta maps out in her signature book is way more than a guidebook for women in business. Marta holds your hand as she compassionately writes about her own journey of self-discovery, which led her to develop the 5-step process mapped out in this book. Marta creates an easy-to-follow process to uncover your strengths, embrace your weaknesses, and forgive yourself for past mistakes so you can transform and be the woman you are here to be to serve the world.

— GINA FONTAINE, One-Minute Wellness Solutions, Health and Wellness Coach, Author, *You Are a Supermom*

In *The Empowered Woman*, not only does Marta share her own path towards empowerment, she offers a concrete formula for others to join her. The book embodies Marta's unique energy, which is equally gracious and supportive and full of life and power. If you're ready to honor your authentic self and build a life that's in alignment,

The Empowered Woman will make your dream future more tangible.

— MELODY GODFRED, Author, *Self Love Poetry: For Thinkers & Feelers and The ABCs of Self Love*

Self-awareness is the key to change, and it is also one of the biggest obstacles in the way of it. In *The Empowered Woman*, Marta gives you a path to understanding yourself in a way that will help not only your business but also your relationships and your sense of self. She ties together past, present, and future beautifully to help you align to the best version of yourself.

— GABY ABRAMS, Success Coach and Certified RTT Practitioner at GabyAbrams.com

For every woman who has wondered if they are worthy of the successful life and business they desire, Marta has shown us that the journey to an empowered and fulfilled life is one that starts within and emanates out into the world. She not only creates an inspiring space with this book, she gives us tactical ways to apply it to our lives. A recommended read for all women in business.

— DANA MALSTAFF, CEO and Founder of Boss Mom at Boss-Mom.com

MARTA SPIRK

THE EMPOWERED WOMAN

THE ULTIMATE ROADMAP TO BUSINESS SUCCESS

Published by
Mom Does It All LLC
Denver, CO
www.MartaSpirk.com

Quantity discounts of this book are available. Personalized autographed copies are also available. Call 1-970-805-0721 for more information and a quote.

The Empowered Woman: The Ultimate Roadmap to Business Success by Marta Spirk

Paperback ISBN: 979-8-9850925-0-9
Library of Congress Control Number: 2021925397

Editing by Melanie Mulhall, Dragonheart
www.DragonheartWritingandEditing.com
Book Design by YellowStudios
www.YellowStudiosOnline.com

First Edition

Printed in the United States of America

This is book is dedicated to my wonderful husband, Shane,

and my gifts to the world: Samuel, Benjamin, and Gloria

CONTENTS

INTRODUCTION

Y OU ARE UNIQUE, AND you are special. My greatest passion is to help you know what makes you distinctive and extraordinary. In taking time to understand my own story and sharing it publicly, I allowed myself to acknowledge that I have a lot of value to give. And so do you.

I'm a mom of triplets, and I immigrated from Brazil to America in 2010. Through the years, I have helped thousands of entrepreneurs to succeed and thrive with my Empowered Woman Path. This path follows the steps that have led to my success and self-fulfillment in business and in life. In walking this path, one of the greatest lessons I've learned is to stop caring whether others approve of me.

I was born on December 2, 1986, in São Paulo, Brazil, and I was the second of two daughters. My parents were well-educated, and my mom had a bachelor degree in English and languages. Originally from Portugal, my dad came to Brazil on a ship at the age of five. His family was quite poor and had come to Brazil to build a new life. On my mom's side, there was money until my grandfather was betrayed by his business partner and lost everything. This resulted in the family moving to São Paulo.

My parents met in a small town in Brazil and got married. They had difficulty conceiving, and once my sister was born, my mom did not want another child. She found motherhood difficult, despite having the support of her parents. I was the big surprise, showing up four years later. My mother was quite religious, first attending the Catholic church and later converting to become Protestant. She said that when she found out she was pregnant with me, God told her everything was going to be okay and the baby would be a blessing.

My mom has said that the lives of everyone in the family improved after I was born, though my sister did not agree with that assessment. As a child, I was very flashy and vocal. My sister lost her only-child status when I arrived, and according to my mom, she became more withdrawn. People frequently reminded me I'd taken my sister's spot and stolen her thunder, so as I grew up, she was the competition in my mind, and I felt I had to earn my place in life. I resented that. My sister also acted as a second mother to me, and I struggled with that for a long time.

My dad's career started to take off after I was born, and he was able to start his own business with a partner who was wealthier than him. That business was in a different city from the one in which we had been living, so we moved to that city and into a house in a wealthy neighborhood. And while my parents lived somewhat frugally, I never lacked for anything.

Throughout childhood, my parents had heated discussions. Even though my father never left the Catholic church, my mother became a pastor and started her own Protestant church. As a small child, I sided with my mother because I was always with her. As an adult, I see that my dad brought a lot of balance to our lives. He was an analytical engineer, while my mother was emotional and impulsive. My father's analytical mind helped him build a very successful business, and he carefully invested his money.

Growing up, I had an intense interest in English. Because of that, people called me "the little American." They would tell me that I didn't even like Brazil and that I wanted to be American. That wasn't true, though. I didn't hate my country. I just wanted to be the best—at everything. That included English.

When my mom got involved in the church, she greeted missionaries who came to Brazil. Because they spoke English, I was fascinated with them, and I loved to impress them with my language abilities. It was satisfying to have these celebrity-like adults treat me with respect and admiration. Later, when I began to interpret and translate, I spent many hours listening to sermons, reading the Bible in English, and comparing the English Bible to the Portuguese Bible. It wasn't assigned in a class. It was something I wanted to do. My end goal was to be recognized as someone incredible.

We will be looking at the Enneagram personality framework later, and my Enneagram type is Type 3, the Achiever, which is said to be the embodiment of American culture. Achievers want to excel in everything. Knowing that I am an Achiever in that system helps to explain how I was growing up. But one of my big disappointments in life is that I have never been great at sports—and the Achiever in me would like to be. My parents didn't encourage me to participate in sports. They were more focused on academics and frequently praised me for being a good student. That alone really attuned me to the American culture.

At fourteen, I started teaching English in my home. Even at such a young age, I was making money from my skills, and without really knowing how much money it was, I gave all my earnings to my mom, saying, "It's for when we go to America." That money actually did go toward helping buy my plane ticket. It was expensive to travel from Brazil to the US. We went two or three times a year to church conferences, mostly funded by the church and partially paid for through my contributions.

It was at one of those religious conferences that I met my future husband. Around the same time, I began college with a major in language and language translation. Languages were effortless for me. I found myself at a crossroads at the time because I was trying to balance becoming an adult, going to college, and being in the church. Having seen the behind the scenes side of the church, I was not interested in continuing on that path, but I still wanted to make an impact in the world and help people. I thought majoring in language would allow me to do those things.

As I studied in college and dated the man who would become my husband, I knew I wanted to live in the US. But everything from friendships to moving away and getting married was affected by both my mom's and my sister's opinions. They were not impressed with my decision to move and marry abroad. Even people in the church told me my future husband was not God's will for me and he was the wrong person for me. That didn't make sense to me. I felt it was my choice. My dad was the only one who supported me in these things, and he was proud of me for breaking free. When my mom locked my things in the closet so I couldn't pack, he was the one who helped me unlock it and pack to go see my soon-to-be fiancé.

Despite the naysayers, my husband and I got married in 2010 and lived in the US for three years, during which time I got my master's degree. It was a wonderful experience to study in the US and be challenged to expand my comfort zone.

Once I'd graduated, my dad convinced us to move to Brazil, so we moved back. We lived there for three years, and it seemed like a good time to have a child. My family was near and there was financial and emotional support for starting a family. But after a year, nothing was happening and the overachiever in me was determined to start a family. There was no leaving it up to chance, so I decided to do something about it. While Latino culture was more about leaving things up to the will of God, my approach was more American: I wasn't going to sit and wait for something to happen.

Seeking help from a specialist was my solution, and it resulted in my having triplets. Over the years, I've learned that I can't wait and leave everything in God's hands because I believe God has already done it all. If there's one thing I took to heart from growing up Christian, it is that Jesus made a way for my happiness and success. They now lay in my own hands and in my willingness to claim them.

The need to earn my place and the feelings and emotions from my childhood really started to bubble up to the surface once I had my triplets. Developing a relationship with my children made me think back to how I felt growing up and what my relationship with my own mom was like.

And what I saw when I did that was I'd grown up with very conflicting information. On the one hand, I'd been told that I was unplanned, which left me feeling unwanted. On the other hand, I'd been told things got better for my family once I arrived. That suggested my arrival had somehow been a blessing to the family. This conflicting information had left me confused growing up. Had I been wanted or not? Was I important to and loved by my parents and sister or not?

The pressure, weight, and responsibility of raising triplets led me to realize I had some self-reflection to do because what I said and did wasn't just going to impact one child, it was going to impact three. I didn't feel I had the luxury to learn as I went along. I was on a quest to be the best mother I could be right away. I was humbled by the thought of it and realized that just as I was trying to be the best mother I could be, my mother had also tried to be the best mother she could be.

The ultimate push for me to start the journey that ultimately became the Empowered Woman Path really happened once my babies were nine months old and we moved back to America. Suddenly I was not only the first-time mother of triplets who would soon become toddlers, I was living far away from the help and support of family and spending several hours a day by myself with my trio of babies.

I came across the opportunity to be a coach in network marketing, and it felt like a good outlet in my new reality. At the time, I had a wonderful woman under me in the network marketing company, and I was able to watch her find herself. She pursued a career as an attorney and eventually created her own online business helping entrepreneurs. While it was wonderful to witness her journey and be a part of it, I still wasn't sure what made me unique or where I was going with my coaching.

With my background as a teacher and in languages, there was definitely a way to use my experience in coaching, but finding direction was key. Before returning to the US, I had worked in an agency that helped Brazilian high school kids apply for American colleges. I helped them write their essays, which included personal statements about what made them stand out as unique. Often, that related to their extracurricular activities and stories from their childhood. That made me start thinking more deeply. I wondered what was unique about me. What could I offer my clients that no one else could?

Before I was able to reach out and help my clients, I had to figure that out for myself. It has been an ongoing process for me, and I believe it is an ongoing process for *everyone*. As long as we're alive, we'll be learning new things about ourselves.

Today I help women entrepreneurs empower themselves by guiding them to see how unique and incredible they are. My focus is helping you find your unique edge—that special thing that is specific to you—and present it in such a powerful way that people will look at you and want to learn from you. This is all about self-awareness and transformation. I call this the Empowered Woman Path. I've put together five steps that will help you find your story within, the distinctive message we all have within us that can change someone else's life: Notice Yourself, Listen to Yourself, Forgive Yourself, Empower Yourself, and Transform Yourself. Through this path, you will learn how to recognize your strengths and your power. You'll learn how you can use those things to impact people and get your ideas out of your brain and into the world.

Are you ready to make an impact? Let's get started!

1

EMPOWERED WOMAN PATH, STEP ONE: NOTICE YOURSELF

*S*UCCESS COMES FROM WITHIN, and this step is all about focusing on yourself and learning who you are without outside approval and reassurance. We're going to look at what makes you unique, what makes you *you*?

I like to tell people that this step is like a crush, the fuzzy warm feeling you get when you start to notice someone and feel you like them. You notice their smile, their eyes, the way they dress, and other personal aspects about them. You need to do this with yourself. Start catching yourself, not just in the mirror, but in everything you do. As you begin to do this, it will become natural. And once you notice yourself, you'll begin to listen to yourself.

Back in Brazil, I worked with students aiming to get into American universities. When I first began, I thought I'd help them with a basic argumentative essay: a thesis, three proof paragraphs, and a conclusion. It wasn't long before I had a rude awakening. Personal statements are actually more like writing a short novel.

For a personal statement, you catch the reader's attention with a narrative stance and then dive into your story. It's something that is quite personal and requires looking seriously at yourself and who you are. That's hard enough when you're a high school student, but if you're older and still haven't figured it all out, it can be even more difficult.

When I started my coaching business, I had to inject my personality into what I talked about to let people connect with me. But I wasn't sure how to be personal, authentic, and unique, which is what everyone in the business coaching field talks about. Business coaches tell you to be yourself and let yourself shine through in your business. But to *be* yourself, you have to *know* yourself. And I realized I didn't know myself.

You may discover that this applies to you too.

I started a business because I wanted to live my life to its fullest potential. To do that, I really wanted to get down and understand who I was and what my purpose was. In doing that, my children would also learn to live their lives to their fullest potentials. Having triplets put a lot of pressure on me. Every mom has mom guilt, and it's totally natural, but with three children growing up at the same time, it really gave me a sense of urgency.

You may be feeling that same sense of urgency to figure out who you are and how to create the best life possible—for yourself, and if you have children, for them too. We're going to start with the Enneagram because I feel it's an important part of noticing yourself.

THE ENNEAGRAM, A PERSONALITY FRAMEWORK

The Enneagram is a personality framework I recommend to all my clients. It has given me an incredible amount of insight into who I am, including my weaknesses and strengths, and it has actually shown me that my strengths are my weaknesses. This is true for everyone. When you don't use your strengths completely and to your advantage, they actually become weaknesses. The whole framework has several layers and is quite complex, but even the basics outlined as follows can be very enlightening.

There are nine Enneagram personality types.
- Type 1: The Reformer
- Type 2: The Helper
- Type 3: The Achiever

- Type 4: The Individualist
- Type 5: The Investigator
- Type 6: The Loyalist
- Type 7: The Enthusiast
- Type 8: The Challenger
- Type 9: The Peacemaker

I'm a Type 3, an Achiever, which is someone who is very goal oriented and who sees their worth in achievements. Achievers look like remarkable people from the outside, but on the inside, there's a lot of emptiness. When all your worth comes from recognition, you have to keep going harder and harder to get your "fix." Unfortunately, like any addiction, you never stop. You just need more and more praise. Learning to no longer need those pats on the back really helped me become more successful.

That was one benefit of discovering my Enneagram type, but there were many other benefits as well, and there will be many benefits for you too. Yes, it can improve your business, but once you understand your lens and start to understand other people's lenses, it can change your relationships. I've seen a big improvement in my relationship with my parents, my husband, my children, and others.

For example, my husband is an electrician. He's very Type 1 (Reformer), so he is blunt and doesn't sugarcoat things. When he starts pointing out all my mistakes, he's not trying to hurt me. He truly wants to help me. Coming from the perspective of a Type 3 (Achiever), it feels like he's trying to put me down because a Type 3 always wants to be praised and recognized for everything they do. By understanding both my Enneagram type and his Enneagram type, I can put what he is doing in perspective. He can do the same thing.

We all see the world through our own lens, and the Enneagram can help us understand what that lens is. The Enneagram will not magically change your personality. It is not intended to do that. What it does is let you understand yourself better, and it lets you understand other people better too. As you begin to grasp your own personality type and the personality types of others who have shared their Enneagram with you, you learn not to take things so personally. You become very clear about who you are, and you can explore that in a healthy way.

Most of us have had the experience of becoming upset by something another person has said to us, sharing that interaction with a friend, and discovering that our friend does not understand why we are upset. In those cases, we may become annoyed with our friend. When we understand ourselves better through the Enneagram, we may be less likely to get upset when someone says something to us that doesn't feel good. And if we relay the interaction to a friend and they don't understand that what was said didn't strike us as positive, we may be less likely to be annoyed by our friend. We understand the nuances of personality in ourselves and others well enough to be more flexible and forgiving about ourselves and others.

Each type has pros and cons. The Enneagram will help you understand the pros and cons of your type by identifying your type and what the strengths and weaknesses of that type are. Every type carries with it a need, and finding that need is a journey. Once you know what you need and figure out why you need it, you can begin to live with yourself in a healthier, more self-accepting way.

If your internal mental and emotional environment is troubled, you will constantly feel you are not good enough. But when your thoughts and feelings are healthy and self-affirming, you realize you have faults and weaknesses, but you love yourself anyway. It's part of who you are, and you can learn to love all of you.

Ready to delve into the Enneagram? To understand and work with what follows, you can begin by taking the test. You can do that (for free) by visiting this website:

www.eclecticenergies.com/enneagram/test

YOUR TEST RESULTS

What Enneagram type are you? Below, I'm going to share information on each type and what some of their weaknesses and strengths are. You may be surprised at just how different you are from other people in your family.

Type 1: The Reformer

People who score a Type 1 on the test are people who never feel things are good enough. They are always trying to improve everything. They're perfectionists, and they are very focused on fixing whatever is in front of them.

Strengths: Type 1s are very loyal. They also take responsibility seriously and often become workaholics. They are ambitious people with lofty goals.

Weaknesses: The fact that perfection cannot be reached means that Type 1s tend to get angry with their perceived shortcomings. They may try to repress the anger, which results in this type behaving in ways that seem critical, judgmental, and annoyed. They get very stressed out and may not let themselves have fun or express emotions.

Type 2: The Helper

Type 2s put their self-worth in how much they can help other people. They tend to be extroverted, and they are the ones who remember special events and care very much about those around them. Type 2s need to be needed to feel good about themselves.

Strengths: Helping others is very much a strength here. Type 2 people are selfless and excellent at distinguishing what other people's needs are.

Weaknesses: Helpers tend to overextend themselves and may burn out, especially if their help is not appreciated. They don't look after themselves as much as they do others, which can lead to breakdowns. In some cases, Type 2s may feel annoyed and become manipulative because they help someone and feel they deserve praise for it.

Type 3: The Achiever

Type 3s require outside validation to make themselves feel good. They are avid pursuers of success and are very goal oriented. They tend to be self-confident and full of energy. They frequently find themselves in social situations and become the center of attention quickly.

Strengths: Type 3s are excellent at presenting themselves and tend to be the people we refer to as self-made. They can become quite successful and are excellent at networking.

Weaknesses: The downside of being an Achiever is that Type 3s need people to praise them. Type 3s often worry that if anyone gets to know them well, they will discover "the truth" about them—some self-identified flaws the Achiever sees in themselves and for which they carry shame deep within them. This can make relationships difficult. They may also find it difficult to find true happiness because they are set on impressing other people, not themselves.

Type 4: The Individualist

This type focuses on creating an identity around being unique. They thrive on individualism and tend to be very complex when it comes to emotions. They are also likely to spend a lot of time in their heads. You will find many Type 4s in artistic careers.

Strengths: Individualists are highly connected to the arts in one way or another, and even if they aren't artists, they appreciate art. They're good at expressing their emotions and tend to be excellent at looking after themselves because they feel they deserve it, due to their feeling that the world is hard on them.

Weaknesses: Type 4s are often self-absorbed and prone to depression. They often feel misunderstood, but they also consider themselves to be better than "common" people. It's very likely a Type 4 will mistake themselves for a Type 5.

Type 5: The Investigator

Investigators are essentially observers. They are comfortable with *thinking* about things rather than *doing* things. Type 5s are generally a little eccentric, and while they like the intellectual side of thinking, they may avoid the emotions that can accompany thought. They're often shy and withdrawn.

Strengths: Type 5s are usually very intelligent and spend a lot of time learning and experimenting. They may be interested in the humanities, science, or arts.

Weaknesses: Type 5s feel weak and sensitive, so they often withdraw from the world. They also are hard to get to know because they keep their feelings hidden, and they very rarely ask for help.

Type 6: The Loyalist

Type 6s tend to have difficulty because they're torn between trusting completely and not trusting at all. They can often be loyal to a fault, continuing on with a job or a relationship even after it is essentially over. The way these people deal with their fear varies on a continuum from being very compliant to being quite defiant.

Strengths: Because they can see a variety of perspectives and potential outcomes, Type 6s are excellent troubleshooters. They like to plan things meticulously and prefer to know exactly what to expect from others.

Weaknesses: Type 6s are very suspicious of new things and people, but they can become overly attached to others if they do begin to trust them. They often have issues with authority because they don't trust authority figures. Type 6s are also prone to worrying constantly and can conjure up every possible negative outcome for a situation.

Type 7: The Enthusiast

Type 7s are focused on living an exciting life and are always on an adventure. They make plenty of plans and tend to be quite energetic. They are often extroverts and tend to be open-minded.

Strengths: Type 7s are excellent entrepreneurs and are enthusiastic enough to get other people involved in whatever they are enthusiastic about. They can be quite successful if they can focus that energy. They are multitaskers and aren't afraid to enjoy life.

Weaknesses: This type of person has difficulty focusing because boredom or any negative feeling makes them uncomfortable. They're always looking for the next best thing and are sure there's a better option around the corner. They are also likely to fall into addictions easily.

Type 8: The Challenger

The challenger is quite determined to be their own boss. Type 8s prefer to be in control of their own destiny and are driven to be successful.

Strengths: Type 8s are well-suited for being the one in control in business, so being entrepreneurs works well for them. They are also fiercely protective of anyone who gets into their inner circle and will be generous with those people.

Weaknesses: This type of person is prone to anger, and it doesn't take a lot to set off a rage. They're also very resistant to authority and can have a hard time showing any type of vulnerability.

Type 9: The Peacemaker

As their name implies, Peacemakers want to avoid conflict and are often active in preventing it. The result is that Type 9s are usually very laid back people who go with the flow and are tolerant of others.

Strengths: Type 9s are excellent parents. As optimists, they see the best in other people and in life, in general. They tend to get along with just about everyone.

Weaknesses: This type of person may undervalue themselves. Because they are trusting by nature, they are more likely to trust someone they shouldn't than other types, and they strive to feel connected to the world to the point of feeling disconnected with themselves.

THE IMPACT OF YOUR CHILDHOOD WOUNDS

Learning to notice yourself and getting to know yourself—including the good, the bad, and the ugly—is a process. It may seem challenging at times, but once you've taken the Enneagram test, you'll start to see yourself in a different light. You'll understand why you behave the way you do.

A client of mine named Jenn commented on how important being "seen" by me had been to her in our work together. She felt that women usually don't give themselves enough credit for how much they have accomplished and don't have a champion to help nudge them on to their next success. Jenn's point about being seen is very poignant. As women, we may find ourselves being skipped over, ignored, or pushed aside.

Often, our beliefs and our values come from events in our childhood. Your personality doesn't develop in a vacuum. It is affected by the people and events around you, and it is important to understand just how that happens. Knowing how you came about and developed is important in and of itself, but it is particularly important if you're starting a business.

As I mentioned earlier, my biggest childhood wound was feeling unwanted, which led to my feeling that I needed to prove my right to take up space in the world. That form of wounding is a very common theme for Type 3s. Each type can be seen as a reflection of unique childhood struggles that became an underlying message influencing who we are as people.

Let's look at some common themes for all the 9 types. As mentioned earlier, each type carries with it a need, so not only is the wounding common for that type talked about below but also the need associated with that type. Note that when I refer to "protective people," I am referring to parents and other authority figures in your life.

Type 1, The Reformer: Self-Judgment

As a child, you may have felt disconnected from the protective people in your life. Lacking guidance and support, you felt the need to become your own judge or critic.

Type 2, The Helper: Self-Sacrifice

As a child, you may have felt a lack of nurturing or structure from the protective people in your life, and to earn their love, you repressed your own needs and became a nurturing figure to others.

Type 3, The Achiever: Self-Rejection

As a child, you may have felt disconnected from the protective people in your life, sensing you were loved only by achieving instead of being loved simply by virtue of your existence. Self-rejection may have resulted from that.

Type 4, The Individualist: Rejection of Identity

As a child, you may have felt very different from the protective people in your life and therefore, misunderstood. The sensation of being "out of place" was very prominent, carrying with it the need to meet someone who finally sees you for who you are.

Type 5, The Investigator: Rejection of Intimacy

As a child, you may have felt disconnected from your family as a whole because you felt different and unwanted, and because of that, you may have sought emotional and/or physical seclusion.

Type 6. The Loyalist: Rejection of Self-Trust

As a child, you may have depended on a protective person in your life for security so much that you failed to develop a sense of security within yourself and trust in yourself. That may have resulted in a constant feeling of fear and uneasiness about the future.

Type 7, The Enthusiast: Absence of Nurturing

As a child, you may have felt disconnected from the protective people in your life because you did not feel nurtured by them. To nurture yourself and self-soothe, you were constantly on the search for the next object or activity that would provide the distraction you craved.

Type 8, The Challenger: Rejection of Childhood

As a child, you may have felt the need to take on the role of a protective person yourself as a way of avoiding showing weakness. The idea of demonstrating vulnerability equaled the possibility of being hurt or rejected, so growing up quickly was the solution.

Type 9, The Peacemaker: Rejection of Your Voice

As a child, you may have felt deeply connected to the people you loved in a way that made it hard for you to differentiate your own feelings from theirs. That means you easily took on someone else's feelings as your own, and to cope with the overwhelm, you learned to tune out negative feelings and situations, pretending they were the norm. You preferred living in denial to experiencing conflict.

As you can see, we are much more than meets the eye, and a part of that is who we are as a result of our childhood wounds. Understanding those wounds is a big step toward healing them because until we understand them, they often impact our behavior in primarily unconscious ways. Knowing how your Enneagram type is related to your wounds helps with that understanding.

UNDERSTANDING YOURSELF IN BUSINESS

You may be wondering why you can't just set up a business and expect to bring in clients. While some companies manage to get a few clients this way, it is not usually a very successful approach. When it comes to business, people don't connect with a company or a concept. They connect with the person within the business. If you're starting a business as a solopreneur, you *are* your business, so you really need to know who you are to effectively share that with your clients. This allows people to connect with you as a person. The best way to make sure that happens is to make yourself human to them, but that can only happen when you've taken a deeper look at yourself and know where you come from.

In business, it's important to treat your clients as unique humans, not just numbers or potential income for you. But the only way to do that effectively is to treat yourself as a person. Because your business is an extension of you, the amount of dedication you put in to your personal development will affect the development of your business relationships and growth.

As stated earlier, success comes from within, and no amount of attention to the external details of setting up a business will make you successful over the long term if you do not understand who you are. But there is no limit to the success you can experience when you not only understand who you are and why you are unique but embrace it fully. That is one of the reasons the Enneagram can be helpful.

SELF-AWARENESS

The first step on the Empowered Woman Path—Notice Yourself—is all about self-awareness. One great tool to help you notice yourself is the Enneagram. If you have answered the Enneagram questionnaire, as I hope you have, take some time to absorb it, integrate it, and decide if the assessment fits for you. Think about a time in your life when one of your Enneagram type strengths was a weakness and another time when it helped you succeed. Contemplate how you manage your weaknesses. And give some thought to how your childhood has helped form the person you are today.

Noticing yourself is the first step on the path. The second step, Listen to Yourself, is also about self-awareness.

2

EMPOWERED WOMAN PATH, STEP TWO: LISTEN TO YOURSELF

*U*NDERSTANDING YOURSELF BETTER IS an essential part of self-awareness, and self-awareness is necessary before you can achieve self-acceptance. You can't accept yourself and give yourself what you need if you don't know what you need in the first place. This step is about listening to yourself, which is another aspect of self-awareness, and you will discover a deeper sense of yourself with it.

You wouldn't sign a contract without reading the entire thing because you wouldn't know what you were agreeing to until you read the contract. This step is similar to reading a contract. In this step, you look back over what shaped you into who you are today and become more aware of the factors that affected you. You get to know aspects of yourself and realize you've basically agreed to be as you are for many years. This step is helpful to check your ego.

When you went through the Enneagram information in the previous chapter, what did you notice about yourself? There may have been some major aha moments there as you realized how you self-sabotage. For most people, it's an eye-opening experience to realize that what you do, what your strengths and weaknesses are, and how you react to things are all related to your personality.

The way you see the world affects everything in your life, from relationships to your business success. Every challenge you are facing right now is happening because of the way you see the world. Everyone has a different challenge because they see the world uniquely and differently from others.

For a long time, my programs focused only on the personal development side of things. They included topics like identifying, embracing, and working through your weaknesses and imperfections. But it goes even deeper when I work with entrepreneurs. Entrepreneurs look at who they are and their unique strengths and weaknesses. Then they go on to monetize them and give back to the world.

ARE YOU LISTENING?

This step, listening to yourself, takes you deeper into self-awareness. You begin to enjoy listening to yourself and understanding yourself, and you make it part of your life. As you begin to listen to yourself, you will notice that *you* are the one keeping yourself from your goals, success, and happiness in life.

Not only are you aware of your flaws at this point, but you are also aware of your strengths—and how your strengths may actually be weakening you. If you're operating in an unhealthy way with your strengths, they can easily become your weaknesses.

I believe I am the only one who can hold me back. This is why I love analyzing what my weaknesses are based on the Enneagram.

You need to listen to your Enneagram type and look at how it manifests in your everyday life. It's also important to listen to the way you talk to yourself. Do you have a lot of negative self-talk? If so, you're going to feel discouraged because you repeat the discouraging, negative thoughts in your head that relate to your type.

As a Type 3, I constantly hear this in my head: *Yeah, you achieved this, but it's not good enough. Go to the next thing to get the praise again.* We all have one form or another of negative self-talk, no matter what our Enneagram type is, but each type has its own way of self-sabotaging. Let's take a look.

Type 1, The Reformer: You missed a spot. It's not good enough. You have to fix the world.

Type 2, The Helper: You didn't help enough. It's your responsibility to make everyone happy.

Type 3, The Achiever: You didn't do well enough. Try harder next time. Keep trying to get praise from others.

Type 4, The Individualist: You're just like everyone else. There's nothing special about you.

Type 5, the Investigator: You're the "odd duck." You don't belong.

Type 6, The Loyalist: You shouldn't trust anyone, including yourself.

Type 7, the Enthusiast: There's something more interesting over there.

Type 8, The Challenger: No one should tell you what to do or try to help you.

Type 9, The Peacemaker: You're worthless and invisible.

When you listen to yourself, you'll notice that nothing is ever enough. These negative thoughts and stories will just keep playing in your head. Listening to yourself creates the habit of monitoring your self-talk. Not only must you become attuned to what you say and how you say it, but you also must become adept at how that relates to your personality type and ultimately, your motives and goals in life. Knowing how we self-sabotage takes our understanding deeper, and that includes becoming aware of our self-talk and catching ourselves in the act of negative thinking and negative self-talk.

CONNECT THE DOTS TO YOUR PAST

Listening to yourself is also a way to connect with your inner child. Take time to look at your childhood more closely and figure it out. You'll come to understand that there were moments in the past when your personality started to show up and where self-sabotage began manifesting itself.

As a teen, I was fascinated with the English language and with music. The variety of emotions that are portrayed in both music and language has always attracted me. There are endless stories and histories connected to these things. I would carry a boombox around the house, set it up near a family member, and tell them, "I'm going to sing and dance now!" Performing was in my blood, but part of it was wanting to prove I was better than my sister.

Because I had heard stories about how my mother didn't want to have a second child and how my sister withdrew into herself after I was born, I had negative self-talk that included telling myself that my mother and sister didn't want me around. It didn't matter that I also heard stories about how our family life improved after I was born. What stuck in my mind was the interpretation that I wasn't really wanted, which meant to me that I had to earn my place in my family. I didn't think I was good enough to be wanted, so I told myself I needed to impress people around me, and performing was a part of that.

It's a good idea to stop and think about your own childhood experiences and how you interpreted them. What are some of the things you constantly tell yourself? Where did they come from? Some of the things in your life and some of the ways you see things in your life are due to your personality type. When mixed with childhood experiences, you create scenarios about the way things were and are. And that impacts the way you see yourself and your world.

We all do this. Our lens is impacted by our personality type and how we translate experiences we had in childhood. That lens impacts how we see and behave in our lives, our relationships, our businesses, and every other aspect of our lives. If you have ever wondered why you attract certain people and experiences in your life, the answer is likely related to what you tell yourself and the lens through which you see the world.

You have a specific world view created from a need you felt as a child that may not have been met. That has now become your reality, but it doesn't have to be that way forever. You can change what you believe, and I'm proof of that.

For me, it was a need to prove I am valuable, I have a space in the world, and I deserve that space. Now I can look back and identify that this need came from my experiences in childhood and the lens through which I saw those experiences. In doing so, my need makes sense. Everyone has something that helped shape who they are today. Looking at your childhood is an important step in identifying that.

You have to realize that the ways in which you self-sabotage haven't just popped up recently. They have been there since you were small, and they were created by beliefs you developed back then. Of course, many things you believed as a child were skewed. As you grow up, you learn new ways to see the world, but certain beliefs are difficult to dislodge. They've been there for years, and that's why they are so difficult to change.

Self-awareness is the beginning of being able to undo the inaccurate and self-sabotaging beliefs that have been affecting you all these years. You don't have to become someone new, but you can become a more self-accepting version of yourself.

Weaknesses are seen as a bad thing because they're the things that can drag you down. However, when you know what your weaknesses are, you aren't victim to them anymore.

It takes a lot of practice to become self-aware. You have to listen to yourself and make a point of noticing your negative self-talk. That can be tough, but it's something you can do if you put your mind to it. When you notice you're being hard on yourself, stop and turn your thoughts to something more positive. The more you do this, the more you'll notice when you self-sabotage. You'll say to yourself, "Oops I'm doing it again." Then you can choose to change your inner thoughts and inner self-talk.

When I push myself too hard and tell myself I need to keep going to prove myself, I catch myself and realize I've done enough and can stop. I can turn off the computer, put down the phone, and stop thinking about it. I don't need to keep trying to impress others. Instead, I can walk away and do some things for myself instead of focusing on others. Of course, it all begins with my thoughts because we think before we act.

That's true for all of us. Long before you make a move, your mind turns things over. Perhaps you feel you are not enough, and then you react to that. If you can catch yourself in those moments when the negative thoughts rear their heads, you can stop them.

BECOMING MORE SELF-AWARE

The more self-aware you are, the more you're able to keep your ego in check. This also allows you to stop your defense mechanisms from popping up. Your defense mechanisms are what get triggered in a particular situation and cause your negative self-talk and self-sabotaging. For example, if you're a Type 2 (Helper) and someone asks for help but you're unable to do anything, you will immediately start to feel you haven't done enough. You feel the need to help, and that can trigger negative self-talk. "I'm not helpful enough. People probably resent me for not doing as much as I should." It can be mentally exhausting.

As a Type 3 (Achiever) with my particular background, my defense mechanism led to this kind of negative self-talk: "You don't love me or want me? I can prove I'm lovable, I'm worthy, and I'm enough! Just let me do another thing. And another thing. Please love me." Now I see the desperate need to be accepted and approved of is what I kept clinging to. It was a piece of my past I enacted automatically whenever I felt unwanted. For most of us, this is a completely automatic response. We've built these habits over the years to resolve what we see as a problem.

Hopefully, you can see how this affects your business. You don't have to constantly look outside yourself for validation or your value in the world. Regardless of your type, you can see yourself as valuable in the world.

In this step, as you are gentler with yourself and more accepting of yourself, you'll see your story and your personality shining through. That makes it so much easier to be authentic. Your expertise is directly connected to your strengths and weaknesses. I feel that your strengths are also your challenges, and we face challenges because we need to overcome them to become more of who we truly are.

SELF-AWARENESS IN BUSINESS

When it comes to business, listening can help you in many ways. As you listen to yourself, you'll learn what your primary skills and expertise are. You can then go on to leverage those skills and use them to help you reach your goals.

I truly believe my expertise is getting a story out of people. My skill lies in helping you learn about yourself and then share your story and use it to create a new future for yourself. I not only do this with others, I do it with myself. I have relied a great deal on external validation, but over time, I have learned to honor my own story. I have grown into a woman who validates herself instead of impressing others to receive the approval she craves.

Each person has experiences that have played a part in forming who they are. Each person has lessons they are meant to learn. And we are each challenged in unique, individual ways. We each have crosses to bear. Our experiences, challenges, and lessons are our personal stories, and they constitute the message we have to share with the world. That message is our gift to the world.

When I met Dawn through a coaching program we were both in, her life and her business were struggling. She had no clarity in her business model and what she wanted to offer, and she was not making much money. Once we started working together, learning she was an Enneagram Type 7 (The Enthusiast) helped her understand that her default patterns and avoiding negative feelings were hurting her ability to feel the range of emotions. This awareness not only impacted her ability to listen to herself to grow her business, but it also helped her emotional eating decrease drastically. She's lost twenty-five pounds and feels much clearer and more joyful about her purpose.

It is critical to unearth and understand our stories—both as individuals and as entrepreneurs. Once we do that, make peace with it, and embrace it, not only can we live empowered, transformed, and fulfilling lives, we can help others do that too as models and as guides.

And an important way we can begin to share our stories and help others understand and share their own stories in business begins with listening to our business audience.

LISTENING TO YOUR AUDIENCE

When you stop to listen to your audience—your clients, your customers, or whomever your business is focused on—and really understand what *they* want to hear about what you have to offer, it changes your business. We tend to get caught up in our own heads and think we know what our clients want, but it may be completely wrong. They have specific things they need to know about your business offering and your skills and expertise. That's what they really need, and it isn't always what you would expect.

I've heard that what is ordinary to us is extraordinary to other people. If this is true, then we may not know what our clients and customers find interesting, important, and extraordinary about us. Listen to your audience and listen to what they praise you about. What they need from you is often very different from what they want to hear or what they see as your strengths.

We often dismiss what we're good at and don't recognize our own greatness—even those who are Type 3 (Achiever) on the Enneagram. It's a very secret and subtle type of self-loathing. Type 3s have a facade of confidence, but there's insecurity behind that. They may not even be aware of the insecurity, but it's there and it affects how they act and speak. Understanding that is where real growth can begin to take place.

This step of listening to others is essential. You need to understand yourself, and listening to what other people say can be one of the keys to that. In fact, it is necessary to understand yourself. When you listen to what others have to say, you learn new things about yourself from an outside perspective. That isn't always fun and pleasant, but when you do that, you will learn more about your strengths and how you can leverage them to help others.

When we are thinking and behaving in unhealthy ways, we all have a modus operandi for dealing with it. Every Enneagram personality type has a specific way of doing that. Type 1s try to fix things. Type 2s try to help. Type 3s try to achieve. And every other Enneagram type has their unique method too. When we're thinking and behaving in healthy ways—just being who we are—we can do what needs to be done instead of falling back on our type-specific defense mechanisms. And that allows us to give our clients and customers exactly what they need.

Remember, while your challenges will never fully disappear, the more self-aware you are—including the more you listen to yourself and listen to your customers and clients—the more you'll improve. No matter how far you advance, you'll see more areas that need improvement. You're always reaching new levels, but you can't do that from a place of self-condemnation. Love your imperfections and love yourself through the challenges.

3

EMPOWERED WOMAN PATH, STEP THREE: FORGIVE YOURSELF

*L*ET'S TALK ABOUT GOING from self-awareness to self-empowerment. If you have done the Enneagram and have done some self-exploration about your background, you are now aware of your shortcomings and challenges. It may be tempting to beat yourself up. Your eyes are opened to your challenges, but you can choose to embrace and love yourself through those imperfections. The second step, listening to yourself, isn't about making you feel bad. It is about helping you be honest with yourself. You can't truly be successful until you understand all parts of yourself.

Beating yourself up over your weaknesses or failures is not a good way to expedite the process. It actually slows the entire process down. In Step 2, you looked at how you self-sabotage. Now it's time to reframe your failures and your mistakes as lessons.

FAILURE = LEARNING OPPORTUNITY

Every mistake you make—and you will make many of them—is a chance to learn. Every time you mess up, you learn what not to do. No one is ever successful without failing multiple times. No one! The difference between successful people and those who are unsuccessful is how they react to those failures. In fact, some people don't even consider them failures. Instead, they count each mistake as a stepping-stone to success.

With every mistake, you're closer to success. Once you realize this, you can make more progress, and that progress will be faster than ever because now that you've learned mistakes can be useful, you will embrace them. You can move forward fearlessly and look forward to the next leap in your learning knowing that nothing—not even yourself—is going to stop you from reaching your goals. Rather than holding yourself back, you'll find yourself leaning in to these opportunities and taking more risks.

Stop for a moment and think about something you wanted to do in your life but quit trying before you accomplished it. Maybe your first attempt failed, so you gave up. How did you react to the failure? What emotions did it evoke in you? Do those reactions and emotions call to mind some childhood experience(s) of disappointment or failure? Now that you have more experience and a different perspective, how would you use that learning opportunity if it occurred now?

GOAL SETTING FOR SUCCESS

Creating goals is the best way to keep yourself moving forward. It's a little like driving in that you have to keep your eyes aimed on the road many feet ahead rather than focusing on what is immediately in front of the hood. If you are looking only a couple of feet ahead, every little thing will stop you, but if you keep your eyes directed on the goal, it's easier to pass those obstacles because you can see the road ahead. No matter what happens, you'll keep moving and taking action.

Life doesn't run smoothly. There are always bumps in the road and difficulties we struggle to overcome. Some obstacles are bigger than others, but that's what life is about, and every person in the world has obstacles. You have to evolve, adjust, adapt, and move forward.

Moving forward may require you to pause for a moment to work things out. You may need to forgive yourself for making a mistake. You may need to forgive someone else to keep going. But do what needs to be done. Then just keep right on going.

This applies to everything in life, but when you talk about business, forgiveness is an important part of the entrepreneurial process. You are going to fail in some or all aspects of your business, but you will learn from those failures. Then you can come back bigger and better than ever.

Once you can accept that your failures are learning experiences and forgive yourself for them, you can extend that same forgiveness to other people in your life, including your clients. Everyone makes mistakes, and when you are able to forgive someone for their mistakes, not only can it help you move on, it also helps them. You have the unique opportunity of being able to guide someone into forgiving themselves and turning their problems into learning opportunities. This method of spreading self-awareness can be a powerful way to reach your audience.

FORGIVENESS AND GRATITUDE

Forgiveness and gratitude go hand in hand. They're also both a choice. Pick someone to think of. It could be a friend, coworker, family member, or even yourself. When you think of this person, you have a decision to make. Will you look at their imperfections and the unpleasant things they've done or will you focus on the positive?

Most of us are more open-minded about others than we are about ourselves. We consider their positive attributes. But we are often less open-minded and harsher on ourselves than we are on others. That's often how human nature works, but it doesn't have to be, and it shouldn't be like that.

Gratitude is part of forgiving yourself. When I took the time to dig up my childhood wounds, I wanted to forgive my sister, my mom, and my dad for their mistakes and imperfections. I decided to look at the positive things they'd contributed to my life and from there, I let myself be grateful for everything they did to help me. This is exactly what we all need! Choose to see the positive instead of focusing on and dwelling on the negative. This is essential in forgiving both yourself and others.

Gratitude for others really starts with you being grateful for yourself. You can't forgive anyone else if you can't forgive yourself for your own mistakes and imperfections. You also can't be grateful to someone else if you're not grateful to yourself and proud of yourself. It all goes back to seeking internal validation and approval instead of seeking external validation.

You are your own best cheerleader, but you must cheer yourself on through everything—both good and bad. If you're trying to improve, you're making progress. Anything you do toward improving yourself is reason to be proud of yourself. Attitude makes a big difference, and not only does it help you feel more confident, it will also help your audience trust you more.

Many people don't realize just how much they're holding on to from their past. You may feel that your emotions and feelings, particularly those that surface when you fail at something, are just a natural response. But in many cases, the origin of those feelings is something that affected you in childhood. Chances are, like me, you have burdens you still carry from childhood.

As a child, I felt the burden of needing to be the center of attention and never dealt with it. Once I was older and that need to be noticed, appreciated, and praised became an obstacle in my business, I had to examine it further. When I was able to let those needs for attention and praise go, I could focus on serving my audience, forgiving myself, and forgiving my family. This has been a journey, and I have not completely mastered forgiveness or gratitude, but I am constantly striving to improve. This couldn't have happened without gratitude for lessons learned. Each mistake I made was a lesson designed to help me learn to move forward in my business.

There's so much love and gratitude in this whole process. You have to learn to forgive yourself, be grateful to yourself, and love yourself. When you do that successfully, your love will expand and you'll be able to love and forgive those around you. As a business owner, this makes a difference to the people you serve. If you're focused on helping others make an impact, it goes beyond you, and it's both incredible and inspiring to see what happens.

It all starts with humility. This is an important part of the journey, and as a Type 3, it is particularly important in mine. I've had difficulty accepting where I am and feeling proud of myself. It took humility to get to that point, and it's an ongoing journey. As I've learned more and more about myself and have managed to create a better vision for my audience, I've also found it easier to help others navigate those waters. The lessons I've learned in life allow me to use my business to help women turn their failures into lessons. And as they do that, they can help empower other women too.

It begins with understanding, forgiving, and loving ourselves instead of looking outside ourselves for those things. When you do that, magic begins to happen.

FORGIVENESS IN BUSINESS

Among the places where that magic will show up is in your business. The more I understood about my childhood wounds, the more I was able to see how they had been showing up in my adult life. Being able to see the connections between my past and present created an urgency in me to heal those hurts so they would no longer impact my present—and my future—in a negative way.

Forgiving my family for what I held deeply within as perceived wrongs allowed me to forgive myself as a person and as a parent. Because our businesses are an extension of who we are, our personal relationships, including anything unhealed from our past relationships, also affect our business interactions. Early on in business, I noticed some negative feelings toward potential clients, mentors, and clients. Those feelings took me back to my school days and the comparison, jealousy, and rejection I experienced in school. I realized that what I had not processed and healed from those earlier experiences was following me into my adult life and impacting my business relationships.

I had no idea starting a business right as I became a mom would be such a double whammy. I faced many emotions about motherhood and business at the same time, and I chose to do something about them for the sake of both my children and my business. I could have become thick-skinned, but I made a different choice. Instead, I softened and learned how to forgive myself and others.

It really was that simple. When you understand the impact resentment can have on your growth as a business owner, you become quick to find ways to overcome it. The benefits far outweigh the pain of letting go of a grudge. By choosing to forgive, you also model this behavior for everyone around you. And since we humans all have flaws, you may find modeling paying off when you need forgiveness too.

FINDING YOUR WAY FORWARD

As I began to teach people the steps on the Empowered Woman Path, I realized something. My own confidence spawns confidence in others. We each have a purpose in life, and as we fulfill it, we help others fulfill theirs. For me, that's teaching you what I've learned over the years. When we see someone who is confident in their authenticity, we tend to be inspired to take action toward fulfilling our purpose, and that is a very powerful gift.

My goal is to inspire you and move you to action. If you aren't inspired to get up and go, then it's not inspiration, it's just admiration. I don't want someone to simply admire me for everything I've done while also having triplets. That's not my goal. My vision and goal is to inspire others to find hope in their own dreams, wishes, and desires. But more than that, I want them to take action on those dreams.

I was so happy when I got my first UK client, Nari. We hit it off, and then I learned she is also an Enneagram Type 3. Understanding her high-achieving traits helped her see how they contributed to her educational and career achievements but had also led to burnout because of her need to remain productive. Once she began practicing the steps on my Empowered Woman Path framework, she reported feeling like a much better friend to herself. As a result of spending more time forgiving herself and getting to know herself better, she experienced a shift in both her personal life and her business. She's been going live on video more often and showing up more confidently when she is on video than she had been in the past. Previously, she'd had difficulty even allowing herself to get on camera because she judged and criticized her appearance and presentation so harshly.

Everything you're learning here is a cycle. You will go through each of these stages over and over. Each time you go through a step, you'll find new insights into yourself.

Remember, this is a journey and it's really one that keeps on going. Teaching these steps does not mean I have mastered them completely myself. I still work through the steps on a regular basis, going through them time and time again. There's always more to learn. Even after you've advanced in your own self-awareness, you will find different levels of self-awareness and self-acceptance.

The most important things I want you to take away from my story and the Empowered Woman Path steps is this: You can continue to work on yourself, and there is no finish line for the project that is you.

4

EMPOWERED WOMAN PATH, STEP FOUR: EMPOWER YOURSELF

NCE YOU ARE ABLE to embrace your imperfections, you are more self-aware, and you can forgive yourself for the things in your life that are not conducive to your growth. No one is perfect. We all have imperfections. Our imperfections help us learn and not only see but also appreciate the good things in our lives.

As they say, there's no light without the darkness, and this applies to life in more ways than one. Now that you understand yourself better (thanks to the Enneagram and your self-exploration) and have acknowledged your weaknesses as well as your strengths, you can better appreciate all aspects of yourself and the good things about your life. Instead of choosing to beat yourself up, you are choosing the paths of forgiveness and gratitude.

And in appreciating who you are by recognizing that all the challenges you have gone through in your life have contributed to being the person you are today, you are finally able to take back your power. When we are in the midst of difficulties, it is tempting to think the world is out to get us. But what if we looked for lessons instead? In my personal journey toward empowerment, the biggest realization has been that all the hurt and pain from the past can only affect me negatively if I choose to give my power away to them through resentment, anger and bitterness.

In revisiting my toughest childhood memories and my family's resistance to my marriage, in stepping up to the challenges of raising triplets, and in developing the self-acceptance and gratitude I've gained through the Enneagram, I have seen that all my experiences have contributed to shaping me and that even the toughest experiences have not destroyed me. This shift in thinking, this reframing of my experiences, has been the most powerful choice about how I see and experience my life that I could have made. And it has made a huge, empowering change in my life.

If being empowered means taking back your power from the things you thought held you back, that means *you* are now in the power seat. You are responsible for your happiness, your success, and everything you desire for yourself and for a fulfilling life. And part of that responsibility begins with controlling what you can control.

OVERCOMING THE VICTIM MINDSET

You are in control of your emotions and your reactions. You are the one who must take responsibility for your actions.

Do you ever find yourself thinking one or more of these thoughts?

- *No one wants to buy from me.*
- *Nobody wants to hear what I have to say.*
- *My spouse isn't supportive enough.*
- *My kids are too needy to let me work.*

These are the thoughts that come from having a victim mindset, from thinking things are happening *to* you. When you start to blame other people or outside circumstances for your place in life, you're giving up. It's time to eliminate that victim mindset. You're not a victim. You are powerful and you have transformed yourself.

You must take control of your thoughts and actions, no matter what you're facing. This is your life, your path, and you are responsible for how it goes. You can't control what other people do, but you can decide how *you're* going to do things. That's where empowerment comes in. You step up to the plate and take control of your own life.

As with everything in life, you have a choice. You can either decide to let outside influences determine what happens with your life or you can focus on your goal and keep going, even if things don't work as easily as planned. Remember that everyone faces obstacles, but the people who keep going are the ones who are successful.

UNDERSTANDING YOUR FEARS

Let's take the victim mentality a step further and get more specific. To overcome it, understanding the forms it can take and the patterns we are up against in our own thoughts can help. Let's look at some of the most common fears that contribute to a victim mentality.

IMPOSTER SYNDROME

Do you feel you're not good enough? Even when people tell you that you are, do you think they only feel that way because they don't know what you are truly like or they will soon realize you don't know what you're doing? This is what we call imposter syndrome.

Imposter syndrome stems from feeling deeply inadequate, and it's surprisingly common. It's also likely you developed it when you were young in response to someone shaming you for your accomplishments or for failing at something you thought you were good at. Whatever the base reason, you need to overcome this and realize you really are good at what you do. What's more, you're the only person who can be *you*, and that makes you unique.

FEAR OF GROWTH

Growth sounds like a great thing, and you may wonder why I would suggest it could be a fear, but many people fear growth. They begin their business with great hope, but then they worry about getting too big. Some of the more common fears include the following:

- What if people think I'm stuck up or better than them?
- If I expand my business, I will need to hire people, and they might cause problems.
- If I make more money, I will have to pay more taxes.
- Everyone will think I'm rich and ask me for things.
- If I make it big, everyone will be watching me and judging me.

There are plenty of things that will happen with growth, but if you're like me, you start to worry about all this long before you actually need to. You may be just starting your business and already worrying about hiring people or setting up foreign offices. That's really just borrowing trouble.

Yes, you should have a plan in place, but you also don't need to stress about growing too fast until it's actually happening. And in the meantime, I highly suggest you work on forgiving yourself and empowering yourself. This will give you the confidence necessary to put yourself out there and really make a difference, not only in your own life, but in other people's lives, too.

FEAR OF SUCCESS

This fear is very similar to the fear of growth. You may worry that if you are successful, something bad might happen. But if you stop and look back at your childhood, you'll likely find the origin of this fear. It could be as simple as finally making the honor roll at school and then falling and breaking your arm. Things like this tend to stick with us, and if you tie making the honor roll to falling and breaking your arm as a child, it can grow into something far bigger than the original event when you are an adult.

Sometimes it's not even an actual event but something people have said. For instance, when I heard my mother say she never meant to have me, it had a massive impact on me as a child—despite the fact that I also heard that life got better in my family after I was born. Words heard in childhood can affect the way you think for the rest of your life unless you do some self-exploration to root out the underlying cause of your fears—like the fear of success.

If you are afraid of success, what has happened in your past that makes you afraid of it? Did something happen or did someone say something? What is the refrain that plays in your mind when you start thinking about being wildly successful at what you love?

With love, gratitude, and forgiveness, you'll find that these fears tend to fade away, and it will be easier to take a step forward.

FEAR OF FAILURE

This is actually one of the most common fears entrepreneurs face, but it can apply to anyone, whether or not they're running a business. Whatever you want to do—lose weight, build a company, raise kids—it can be terrifying to think of what will happen if you fail. But as we've already discussed, failure is a learning opportunity.

The trick here is to push through the fear. Review Step 3 and consider what you can gain if you fail and try again. Every failure is a lesson to be learned, and that puts you one step closer to your goal. Another thing that can help is to ask yourself what the worst thing that can happen is. If things go terribly wrong, what are the consequences?

Often, what you're really worried about is the *idea* of failure and not the *actual* failure. Even if you worry that other people will see you falter, know that most people are so focused on themselves that anything you do will be a blip on their radar. And if they're stuck on your mistake while you keep moving on and reaching for your goals, they may stay stuck while you move forward and become successful.

DON'T LET YOUR FEARS SLOW YOU DOWN

Each of these fears is very common, but that doesn't mean you need to let them stop you or even slow you down. If you find you're hesitating to create the life you want, then you need to start looking at forgiving yourself and those in your past. Then you can focus on gratitude and building yourself up.

CELEBRATE YOURSELF

As you worked through the previous steps in the Empowered Woman Path, you opened the door and turned the light on to some of the things in your behavior that don't serve you. You've probably discovered some of the patterns you've had since childhood, and you've looked closer at how those patterns developed. It can be a bit disconcerting to realize that some of your life is based on beliefs that were created as defense mechanisms or coping methods in response to things that happened and were said many years ago. But you need to understand those patterns and behaviors in yourself to overcome them.

Now it's time to celebrate who you are and be proud of yourself. This is a choice you need to make on your own. I can tell you to be proud of yourself, but it has to come from inside *you*, and that all begins with forgiveness and gratitude, which you explored in the third step and which should be an ongoing process.

You've overcome so much in life and accomplished an incredible amount. You're not depending on others to give you validation from the outside. Instead, you now understand that you must recognize the greatness within yourself. Everything that comes from others is a bonus.

At the same time, it's very common to still struggle with external obstacles, and you may realize at this point that lows are never going to go away. The negative feelings and emotions you experience will not simply vanish one day to never return. What changes is your response to them. That is where your attitude really comes into play.

You are allowed to feel the feelings and process the emotions, but then you need to pick yourself up. You don't have to rely on others to lift you up off the ground. They may not always be there when you need them, but you always have yourself.

At this stage, you've learned to self-validate. You know you're valuable and can be successful, but you may still be allowing other people's opinions to affect how you see and feel about yourself and your business. You must trust yourself and empower yourself. Get clear on your core values. What do you want to be known for? You've become aware of your unique power and authenticity, and now it's time to trust them.

You know what your strengths are and where success lies for you, thanks to the Enneagram test you took in Step I. Now you need to embrace them. Celebrate yourself. Remind yourself of your greatness. Create affirmations for yourself and repeat them every day!

EMPOWERMENT IN BUSINESS

I can't say it enough: Your business is an extension of you. And now that you know what empowerment is and recognize the need for forgiveness and gratitude, you can use these things in your business dealings. As an empowered person, you are also an empowered entrepreneur who can empower others. Whether you realize it or not, your products and services have the ability to change someone for the better. The most important thing for your business growth is not only understanding *how* your business empowers people, but also conveying it clearly so potential clients see the value of your work and decide to invest in what your business has to offer.

The most beautiful part of recognizing that you empower your clients through your business is this: The more you remind yourself of that, the more you believe it. And the more you believe it, the more your clients and customers believe it too. It's a wonderful cycle of contagious empowerment! By empowering yourself and reminding yourself of your expertise and credibility, you can more clearly convey why your target market needs your product or service because you truly are the expert in whatever your business offering is. And when an expert is making their offer to the world, those who buy their products or services are elevated—empowered—through that offering because whatever was holding them back that your product or service can address allows them to soar in a new way.

But if you feel like an imposter and haven't yet mastered overcoming that, I suggest you look at the people you've already helped in your journey. Even if you haven't yet got a product or service to market, you've helped people. Chances are, you chose your business for a reason. Maybe people told you how much you helped them or you simply realized you were doing the same thing over and over again and doing it well. Either way, this is the perfect time to use that knowledge to build yourself up. Then turn around and offer your expertise to those who need it.

Getting in the habit of talking about your products and services is extremely important when it comes to building up your confidence. The more confident you feel, the more trust you earn with potential and current clients. They'll see you moving forward, and your self-empowerment will encourage them to work with you or purchase from you. This is what I like to call Empowerment Marketing because it is just as much for you as it is for them. Repetition of the benefits of your business is as important for you as it is for those you seek to help, but to reach that point, you have to get into the habit of empowering yourself as both a person and a business owner. For that, I have a tool I first heard of from one of my first mentors, and I highly recommend: a brag book.

You may have heard of the power of a gratitude journal, but if you use one, have you noticed that *you* are hardly ever in it? My suggestion is to keep track, preferably daily, of the things you are proud of having accomplished, big and small, and watch how this gratitude for *yourself* unfolds in more success and empowerment.

When I first started working with Rubecca, she had started a side hustle that was booming. After fumbling around a bit on her own, she was guided by a friend's social media post to one of my free online events. During this free event, one of my sons was banging on the door and yelling in the background. I was mortified and felt unprofessional, but later, Rubecca told me that seeing me excuse myself from the meeting to address my family's needs and return like nothing had happened was her "this is for me" moment. As a working mom, having a coach who understood *exactly* what her reality is like was what she was looking for.

Rubecca went on to apply my Empowered Woman Path tools and strategies and often texted me her little wins. It was her version of a brag book! As someone who tended to keep success a secret, the encouragement to take notes of her celebrations, plus having someone to share them with, proved to be fun and inspiring for Rubecca. It opened up a new way for her to experience relationships with others, one in which people cheer each other on rather than compete.

By keeping track of the things she's proud of, Rubecca empowered herself to quit her full-time job and now has her own team of professionals working for her at her Pilates studio. This is the power of celebrating yourself by writing down and sharing your wins.

All the steps on the Empowered Woman Path build on each other: As you learned more about yourself, your personality, and your self-talk and then intentionally chose to forgive yourself and others, you became fully capable of embracing all of yourself. You can now intentionally choose to celebrate all you are and have to offer without guilt and shame. And in doing that, others can benefit from your empowerment and gifts. You have transformed from a caterpillar into a beautiful, self-accepting, and unique butterfly.

5

EMPOWERED WOMAN PATH, STEP FIVE: TRANSFORM YOURSELF

*W*HAT HAPPENS WHEN YOU transform yourself? It's not just something that helps *you*, it also helps your *business* and changes everything around you. Even the *people* around you will be affected.

My hope is that going through the process of working through the steps on the Empowered Woman Path is a transformational experience, not in the sense that you're re-inventing yourself or becoming a whole new person, but rather that you're simply becoming a more self-accepting version of yourself. After noticing, listening to, forgiving, and empowering yourself, you are able to exude more of your authentic self than ever before.

For a variety of reasons, we often hold ourselves back from becoming all we can be. Maybe you're trying too hard to impress everyone. Of course, you will never be able to do that because it is impossible to impress *everyone*. Maybe you want to help people, but you never feel you do enough to help. The way we hold ourselves back is heavily affected by our Enneagram type. It's time to stop holding yourself back and start becoming more of who you were always meant to be.

Many people want to skip straight to the transformation part of things, but we're covering it last for a reason. This is the final step in the process because it is the culmination of the other steps. You cannot get to transformation without having worked through the four steps before it. Once you have completed this step, you will find it easier to reach your goals. Anyone can set a goal, but if you're setting them while coming from an interior place of self-hatred or because you are unhappy, you are going to set very different goals than you will set if you are self-aware, self-accepting, and empowered. You'll also go about reaching them differently than you will if you have worked through the five steps. This is why I have developed the five steps on the Empowered Woman Path.

At this stage, you are able to authentically say and mean some things that would not have been true about you if you were not as self-aware as you now are:

- "I know I can't be anyone but myself."
- "I've learned to make my weaknesses my biggest strengths."
- "I behave in healthy, functional ways."

All the work you've done on the Empowered Woman Path has helped you embrace all of yourself, but as I have said previously, the journey doesn't stop there. Here are some ways to keep stepping into your authentic, empowered self.

SURROUND YOURSELF WITH LIKE-MINDED WOMEN

Sometimes you may feel lonely or burnt out on this journey. There are some great ways to help prevent this, and surrounding yourself with like-minded women is one of them. That's because our friends are a massive influence in our lives. They can either add fuel to help propel you forward into success or they can drag you down.

Few things are as depressing as someone who doesn't have confidence in you and doesn't understand your choices. It is difficult—and sometimes impossible—to discuss your business ideas with them because they will be unable to share your vision enough to be good sounding boards, let alone supportive and encouraging. That does not promote personal growth and self-awareness. But if you surround yourself with like-minded women, you'll find that you are encouraged and inspired to keep digging deeper into yourself.

When I first met Kelsea through a training I presented on the Enneagram, we instantly connected because she's also an Enneagram Type 3. I invited her to one of my Empowered Woman School meetings, and she burst into tears when she joined me and the other women there. Having a community of incredible women cheering each other on and giving useful feedback felt like coming home to her. She decided to join the program. She confided in me that being a part of a group designed to build each other up was priceless to her, and it has been crucial in helping break down many of the old business models she had been carrying around, including those involving competition, jealousy, and negativity.

How do you find these like-minded women? Where are they? You can look for them in many places including online business groups, local business meetups, classes, mastermind groups, and even among your friends and within your family. One of my goals has been to create these types of communities myself to cultivate a container of support and empowerment. And if you feel called to do so, start your own group too.

CREATE ACCOUNTABILITY

Creating accountability is important to keep yourself on track and is important in your relationships with your clients and customers. If you are holding yourself accountable and being held accountable by others, you're more likely to keep going through the tough spots. It's like exercising when you just don't want to do it. If you're left to your own devices, you might decide to skip the exercise and just veg out, but if you have a running date with a friend, you're going to show up because they expect you to be there. That's accountability.

You don't necessarily need to have someone else keeping tabs on you all the time. There are numerous types of accountability.

- **Personal Accountability:** With personal accountability, you function on your own and keep track of your own progress. You can use a calendar or journal to keep up with your progress, but even a sticker chart or rewards program you design with your end goal in mind can work well.
- **Public Accountability:** Another option is to let the world know what your goal is. Shout it to the sky!

Post it on social media. Let your friends and family know. Then the knowledge that people are watching will keep you moving forward. This can also be a great way to connect with your potential clients and show them how you are working to improve.

- **Group Accountability:** Forming a group or joining one that has a similar purpose can aid you in building up some accountability. This is a good method to use with your ideal clients if it fits your brand. For example, a fitness group might meet in person or online, and everyone posts their goals and updates the others regularly.

- **Friend and Family Accountability:** Friends and family may also be able to help you with accountability. But you really need to find the right people in your circle and make sure they are of a similar mindset or you'll find yourself being held back.

- **Coaching Accountability:** Personal, public, group, and friend accountability can make a big difference, but if you really want to take yourself and your business to the next level, having a mentor you can talk to and who understands you enough to kick your butt when you need it can be instrumental in getting you there. Think of this as a personal trainer for your mind. You can hire someone who meshes with your ideas and is able to check in with you throughout your journey to ensure you are moving in the right direction. They can also help you troubleshoot where necessary.

You can even use multiple ways to increase your accountability, but any method you use should result in inspiration, not disheartenment.

KEEP INVESTING IN YOUR GROWTH

You should never stop learning. In fact, it's been shown that if you continue to learn on a daily basis and pick up new skills, you actually protect your brain against diseases like Alzheimer's and other forms of dementia.

There are many ways to invest in your growth. I love brainstorming this with people because everyone has their own ideas about what constitutes growth for them and how to accomplish it. As long as you make sure you're always growing and learning, there are endless possibilities. Age doesn't matter. You can always learn new things.

Reading books is a good way to start out, and it costs very little if you use the library or a service like Kindle Unlimited. Find the right books for your needs.

Continue with coaching even if you've already grown a lot. The right coach will help you grow your goals and aspirations as you continue to develop.

Another area you can continue to grow in is self-knowledge. You're going to listen to yourself from here on out—and not just how your body feels, but what is going on in your mind. When you slow down for a moment and think about what you're reacting to and how you're reacting to, you can hone your ability to respond instead of just react.

TRANSFORMATION IN BUSINESS

Just as making the personal changes in the first four steps also changes your business, transforming *yourself* also transforms your *business*. Your business is organic and alive like you, and as you grow, your business grows. There's no way around it, and the fact of that is all the more reason to invest in your personal growth. Among other things, it means that as you step into new levels of authenticity, your products and services—and even your target audience—may evolve and transform. It is very common for business owners to change direction and experiment with new ideas in their entrepreneurial journey. Don't let that make you feel like a failure because it is a normal and integral part of the process. In fact, I encourage you to learn about the histories and stories of successful businesses in your industry and other industries because when you do, you will see that success is rarely a linear process.

I also urge you to get in the habit of reframing failure by understanding that every perceived misstep is actually a stepping-stone helping you get closer to your ultimate destination. And when you embrace your personal journey as something unique, the temptation to compare your mile marker to someone else's will fall away. Yes, we need points of reference, but only to help encourage us to keep going, not to make us feel we're constantly behind.

And finally, know this: As you empower yourself and transform, you'll become someone else's point of reference. Your story of empowerment and transformation will serve as encouragement for those with whom you come in contact.

CONCLUSION

*N*OW THAT YOU HAVE gone through my Empowered
Woman Path five-step process—Notice Yourself, Listen to Yourself, Forgive Yourself, Empower Yourself, and
Transform Yourself—you should be in an excellent position
to create an empowered woman life and business reality.

You have gone from paying attention to yourself and noticing yourself to understanding your Enneagram type.
You've learned who you are and why you act the way you
do. You've identified your weaknesses and have learned
that just because you have a weakness (we all do), that
doesn't mean you're doomed. In fact, your weaknesses can
easily become strengths. Your fears are no longer as strong
as they once were, and they've lost their hold as you've
gained the courage and confidence to move toward your
goals, regardless of the obstacles in the way.

You've learned to listen to yourself and to look at where
your negative self-talk comes from. You've come to understand that we often have voices from our past that

reverberate in our heads, making us think and act in less than optimal ways. With more self-awareness, you've learned how to translate all of this into your business context and to reach out to your audience and empower them.

The power of forgiveness has been shown, and hopefully, you've embraced that. This may be one of the most difficult steps, particularly when it comes to forgiving ourselves. Now that you've learned to forgive, gratitude opens up to you more fully. With gratitude for yourself and others, you are ready to head toward your goals. Set your goals from a place of gratitude and watch how quickly you reach them. From there, you've learned that by embracing and celebrating all that you are, you truly are empowering yourself and, therefore, empowering others around you. And finally, you've seen how all four steps culminate in increasing levels of self-acceptance as you allow yourself to step into who you really are, knowing you are good enough to pursue your dreams and help others do the same.

The five steps on the Empowered Woman Path are a continuing cycle because learning and growth is a continuous cycle. Even though I devised this five-step method, I still use it and work through it endlessly because there's no point at which I think I'm perfect and won't benefit from additional growth. It's a process, and there's always room for more growth, more transformation, and more forgiveness.

Each time I work through the steps of this process, I discover and learn more about myself and the world around me. I learn to appreciate different nuances within my life story and my purpose. You will too. It's similar to repeated viewings of a favorite movie. Even though you know what is going to happen, you pick up on new things each time you experience it. But instead of watching a movie for entertainment, you're actually upgrading yourself, your life, and your business in a way that impacts those around you more than you can ever know.

It isn't always comfortable to keep digging deep into your memories and your past, particularly when you explore how negative behaviors began. It can be painful and unpleasant, but that is what allows you to forgive, be grateful, grow, and transform.

WHAT'S NEXT?

You haven't reached the end of your journey by any stretch of the imagination. Even if you've taken your time moving through each step, more growth and transformation are available to you as you continue to work with this process. In case you haven't realized it yet, I'm always pushing for more improvement. It's the best way to get what you want out of life!

So now that you have completed the five steps, I encourage you to go back to the beginning and start over again. Enjoy your transformation and make note of how it has impacted your personal and business relationships. Begin paying attention to how you and your personality differ from those you interact with. Investigate your triggers and whether you have been able to avoid taking things as personally as you did before you began this process. Make a point of reminding yourself that you are in the power seat of your life. You may not have realized that before you stepped onto the Empowered Woman Path, but you do now. And you certainly know more about yourself and your story than before, and you understand that you are irreplaceable. Consider carefully what you will do with all this newfound information.

And be empowered!

ACKNOWLEDGMENTS

I want to thank my Lord Jesus, who loved me first and showed me what love is so I could love myself and others.

My deepest gratitude to my parents, Fernando and Ana Maria. You are exactly the father and mother I needed to become the woman I am now.

Many thanks to my sister Denise, my best friend and confidant since birth.

Thank you, Shane, my soul mate, for challenging me to find my voice by seeing and showing me the world in such a different way. I am so grateful I followed my heart and didn't listen when everyone else doubted our relationship. You are truly my rock.

Thank you, Sammy, Benny, and Gloria for being my answered prayer. You have been the biggest gift to help me step into my calling.

Thank you, Dana Malstaff. Your group was a beacon of hope when I doubted I could be a (triplet) mom *and* a business owner. Thank you for paving the way for moms to follow their dreams.

Rebeca Storck Lima, your faith in Jesus and in me were paramount on this journey. I know for a fact he brought us together, and the best is yet to come. It gets better and better.

Christina Nicholson and Lisa Simone Richards, you are the best power team I could have asked for when I had no idea where I was taking my business. Following my heart to gain visibility really taught me so much more about myself than I could have imagined. You are brilliant!

Natalie Tysdal, your warmth and reassurance meant so much to me as I was finding my footing in growing my business. Your beautiful heart and welcoming smile always remind me I can do hard things.

Gary Barnes, no words could really do justice to all the love and guidance you have given me. I will be forever grateful that you took me under your wing when I felt lost and helpless. You have literally been like a father to me. Thank you from the bottom of my heart.

Gaby Abrams, consider this book one of the many ripple effects of your decision to start anew. Thank you for showing me I could be myself and find success. Latina divas unite!

Genesis Blue Davies, when we met online, I would have never imagined you would become a key player in getting this book out. I am so grateful for your help in getting my thoughts and words out of my head and onto paper.

Veronica Yager, thank you for all your help and patience in making this dream come true. Get ready for a second book!

Melanie Mulhall, thank you for sharing this beautiful experience with me and making sense of my thoughts to produce the best finished product I could have asked for. You are more than an editor, you are the refined voice in my head and heart.

All my love to my clients and friends who have truly made all of this possible. Thank you for allowing me to be a part of your world. Without you, none of this would have come to be.

To all the members of The Empowered Woman School and my other programs: You are the definition of Empowered Women. Remember that.

Finally, as a true Type 3, I want to thank everyone who went out of their way to express their support for me and my work throughout the years. It has not gone unnoticed. I cherish all your loving words and compliments more than you could imagine. So, thank you! *Obrigada*!

ABOUT THE AUTHOR

Born and raised in Brazil to an entrepreneur dad and a pastor mom, Marta demonstrated an interest for the English language and American culture very early on and began teaching English at fourteen.

She went on to get bachelor's and master's degrees in English, became a certified court interpreter, and married an American she met at a church conference in Tulsa, Oklahoma.

After the surprise and blessing of triplets in 2016, Marta found a passion for encouraging and empowering women as she learned to encourage and empower herself through the challenges of adult (and triplet) life.

In 2020, her dream of becoming a US Citizen finally came true, and her coaching business grew exponentially. She now serves thousands of entrepreneurs, helping them to stop spinning their wheels by trying random personal development resources and finally learn to boost confidence and grow their business by looking at their most valuable resource: themselves!

A NOTE FROM MARTA

I hope this book encouraged you in your personal and entrepreneurial journey. If you would like to know more about my work, go to www.martaspirk.com. And if you would like to share how the book has made a difference in your life, please write to me. I'm always excited to read your personal stories. You can reach me at contact@martaspirk.com.

READY TO HEAR MORE?

If you're ready for more inspiration and ideas, you can find them on Marta's podcast, *The Empowered Woman*, anywhere you listen to podcasts or on iTunes:

https://podcasts.apple.com/us/podcast/the-empowered-woman-personal-growth-visibility/id1404493563

A POSSIBLE NEXT STEP WITH MARTA

Marta has created a unique program called *The Empowered Woman School*. This is a membership program to enhance personal and business growth for women entrepreneurs. It is designed to give you content, coaching, and community as a form of accountability in the implementation of the Empowered Woman Path and to provide specific strategies to grow your business. As a reader of this book, you are now a part of the Empowered Woman family and eligible to claim a 30-day free trial to the school.

Go to www.freegiftfrommarta.com to get started.

Be empowered!

MARTA SPIRK IS THE IDEAL PROFESSIONAL SPEAKER FOR YOUR NEXT EVENT!

Marta Spirk is an international speaker who has appeared on KWGN-TV and KDVR/FOX31 Denver and on worldwide podcasts and events. Her high energy and impactful message will inspire your audience, and she will leave them empowered to take action. Marta uses the power of stories to encourage everyone to live an empowered life by seeing challenges and adversity as lessons and stepping-stones to create their desired reality.

Marta's Most Requested Programs

- **Boss Mode Through the Enneagram: Turning Your Weaknesses into Your Superpower**
- **Using Your Love Language on Yourself: Stop Seeking External Validation and Nurture Yourself**
- **The Power of Empowerment Marketing: Master Your Content and Magnetize Your Ideal Clients**
- **Get Seen, Gain Trust, and Get Paid: Engage and Serve Your Audience in 5 Easy Steps**
- **Step Up, Speak Up & Show Up: Identify and Overcome Fears to Make Confidence a Habit**

If you would like to know more about booking Marta for a keynote, breakout session, or workshop, please contact us by calling 1-970-805-0721. You may also e-mail your questions to contact@martaspirk.com.

SHARE THIS BOOK!

Quantity discounts of this book are available. Call us at 1-970-805-0721 for more information and a quote. Personalized autographed copies are also available.